LET THERE BE VIRTUES

A book for African American adolescent girls ages 10-15 years old.

Bernetta "Breezy" Watson

authorHOUSE®

AuthorHouse™ LLC
1663 Liberty Drive
Bloomington, IN 47403
www.authorhouse.com
Phone: 1-800-839-8640

Published by AuthorHouse   07/26/2014

ISBN: 978-1-4969-2865-8 (sc)
ISBN: 978-1-4969-2864-1 (e)

Library of Congress Control Number: 2014913095

Any people depicted in stock imagery provided by Thinkstock are models,
and such images are being used for illustrative purposes only.
Certain stock imagery © Thinkstock.

KJV
Scripture quotations marked KJV are from the Holy Bible, King James Version (Authorized Version). First published
in 1611. Quoted from the KJV Classic Reference Bible, Copyright © 1983 by The Zondervan Corporation.

DEDICATION

Adolescence

The state or process of growing up. Life from puberty to maturity. Youthful, growing into womanhood.

To Jazmine Watson and Jiamond Watson, my granddaughters

And all African American adolescent girls.

1 Timothy 4:12

Don't let anyone look down on you because you are young, but set an example for the believers in speech, in life, in love, in faith and in purity.

CONTENTS

INTRODUCTION

Being and adolescent is a wonderful time in life. You will have the greatest growth and development since being an infant then a toddler you will learn how to take care of your personal appearance and personal hygiene, becoming an adolescent carries a great responsibility you must learn social skills, life skills, manners, etiquette, communication skills and table manners. You will develop virtues, morals, spiritual awareness, positive self-esteem, and positive self-confidence. You set goals, stay focus on your future and learn leadership skills, you will lead by example. Say no to drugs, alcohol, sex, peer pressure and bulling.

Your future is bright and promising, stay in school, get help if you need help with your school work you can go to your parents, teachers, counselor and you can get a tutor.

Extra curricular activities like dancing, singing in the school choir, playing a sport, joining a book club or starting a book club. You can learn to play a musical instrument it could be rewarding. Exercise keep your body fit and eat a healthy diet, drink enough water. Get yourself a hobby or start a small business. Just get busy and stay focused.

INTRODUCTION

Galatians 5-22, 23

The Fruit of the Spirit is Love, Peace, Long Suffering, Gentleness, Goodness, Faith, Meekness, and Temperance against such there is no law the meaning of fruit is significant for three reasons it means the result, product, outcome or effect produced by the Spirit in the believer's life.

As fruit on a tree takes time to grow and mature, so Spirit does not cultivate these virtues in the believer's life overnight.

Virtue is goodness and a beneficial quality, moral excellence.

Proverb 31-10

The words of King Lemuel, the prophecy that his mother taught him. Who can find a virtuous woman? For her price is far above rubies.

It is God who has made us not we ourselves. You are wonderfully made and loved by him.

You are a child of Gods and no one can change that.

INTRODUCTION

Meaning of Adolescence

Adolescence is a time for growth and development.

This book will help give you important information about being an adolescent. Adolescence is a time for body growth but it is also a time for moral growth.

Virtues are defined as general moral excellence, upright goodness. Knowing the right things to do. Making wise decision about your conduct and behavior. A time to focus on your educational goals. Be a leader not a follower, avoid peer pressure and bulling.

GROWTH DEVELOPMENT
AFRICAN AMERICAN ADOLESCENT GIRLS

Growth and development of African American adolescent girls, need physical, social, religious, emotional, educational and intellectual development to become a whole and complete adult.

Black churches will continue to be a place for adolescent black girls to get support for their growth and development.

Adolescence is the period of growth from puberty to maturity.

Early adolescence, also known as pre-adolescence, which usually begin between ages of 10-15 years old.

Pre-adolescent females become focused on their physical changes. Their preoccupation with themselves may result in them behaving in a self-conscious way. They will take increased amount of time getting dressed, taking great interest in make-up, body fragrance and lotion. They become interested in boys.

This is the girl's most rapid growth since infancy. There is a growth in height, first pubic hairs, under arm hair, budding breast and menstruation usually happens.

SOCIAL SKILLS

Social skills are learned behavior, social skills are the skills we us to communicate and interact with other people, verbally, nonverbally through gestures, and our personal appearance.

A person who uses good social skills is a respectful person, who does not interrupt when others are talking, a person who is kind, well mannered, and polite and speaks in calm tone of voice, avoid conflict and is not verbally abusive.

When you have good social skills you know how to use your communication skills, you have the ability to listen then respond, you will know which conversations to talk about and which topic to avoid talking about.

It will not be easy all the time when we are interacting with others, these are the times that you must be patient and make a great attempt to communicate and interact in a positive manner.

Sometime you will commit a faux pas which is a social error, you might say something that is not nice about a person not knowing the person that you were talking about heard you talking about them, the way you correct that social blunder, you apologize and keep going.

MAKING A GOOD FIRST IMPRESSION

First impressions are lasting impressions. It is almost impossible to change a first impression. When you meet someone for the first time they will make an assessment of who they think you are. Their visual assessment only takes 3 seconds, they make their assessment by way you are dressed, the way you talk, walk, sit, stand, body language and your mannerism.

You will be judged by the way you communicate with your peers and others. You only get one chance to make a good first impression.

Inspirational Reading taken the King James Bible

Ecclesiastes 3: 1-8

Soloman reflects on all of life he expresses in a beautiful poem of 14 opposite events that God has a sovereign design behind all events.

The meaning of sovereign is exercising or possessing supreme jurisdiction or power. [taken from the Webster dictionary.]

1. To everything there is a season and a time to every purpose under the heaven.
2. A time to be born and a time to die; a time to plant and a time to pluck up that which is planted.
3. Time to kill and a time to heal. A time break down, and a time to build up;
4. A time to weep, and a time to laugh; a time to mourn, and a time to dance.
5. A time to cast away stones and a time gather stones together a time to brace, and a time to refrain from embracing.
6. A time to get and time to lose; a time to keep, and a time to cast away;
7. A time to rend, and a time to sew; a time to keep silence and a time to speak.
8. A time to love, and a time to hate; a time of war, and a time of peace.

MEANING OF GOOD MANNERS

Good manners are the treatment of other people with courtesy and politeness and showing correct public behavior.

Good manners are acting in a way that is socially acceptable and respectful with consideration for others.

Good manners are doing unto others as you would have them do unto you. Matthew: 7-12

Saying thank you, please, you are welcome, excuse me, and good morning with a smile are words used when we practice good manners. Always speak when you enter a room.

MANNERS AT HOME

Good manners at home begin with respecting your parents and everyone that lives in your home.

Help with the household chores as assigned by your parents.

Use good table manners at home. You can also help clean the table and the dishes after dinner. Be polite at home always remember to say please and thank you.

When you go out to visit a friend or relative always come home the time your parents have instructed you, please always call if your plans change, keep your parents informed of where you are. Call home for a ride, never leave out alone, and be safe.

MANNERS AT SCHOOL

1. Obey all school rules.
2. Arrive at school on time.
3. Go to your classes on time.
4. Do not miss school unless you are sick and have permission from your parents.
5. Turn in all your homework and special assignments on time.
6. Use your indoor voice in school.
7. Raise your hand when you would like to be recognized by your teacher.
8. Wear causal clothes to school always be neat and clean.
9. Be always aware of body and your personal hygiene, no body or underarm odor, take bath and be sure to use your deodorant.
10. Brush your teeth and use mouth wash daily before going to school so you can prevent bad breath.
11. Always have good manners and social skills on the school bus.
12. Do not chew gum in school.
13. Use your good table manners at lunch time.
14. Play fair on the playground with your classmates.
15. Always respect your teacher and all the school staff.

MANNERS AND ETIQUETTE
ON THE SCHOOL BUS

1. Obey all rules of the bus
2. Stay in your seat until you reach school or home
3. No eating, drinking sodas or juice on the bus
4. No loud noise or loud talking
5. No playing around or fighting on the bus
6. No radios or cells phones
7. Obey the bus driver

CHURCH MANNERS AND ETIQUETTE

1. Make sure your personal hygiene and personal appearance are A+ when you go to church.
2. Make sure your shoes and stocking match.
3. Check yourself out in the mirror before leaving home for church.
4. Always take your Bible to church.
5. No chewing gum, no eating in church.
6. Do not use your cell phone in church, no texting, no playing games
7. No talking in church or writing notes to your friends.
8. Never walk while the minister is praying or delivering the sermon. If you need to go to the bathroom you may walk and the usher will direct you to proper exit.
9. When you accept an assignment like the praise dancer, choir, ushers or a youth group, be on time. Attend all meetings and practices if you cannot attend call your leader and let them know that you will be late or you cannot make it to the meeting.

LIBRARY MANNERS AND ETIQUETTE

Use your indoor low tone voice in the library, it is a quiet zone. Students are reading, studying and completing their homework assignments. There will also be library user that are there for the quiet atmosphere and the relaxation of reading a good book. You will find all types of magazines, news papers, CD's, Talking books and much more an example is the computer lab and you can get assistance any time you need help just ask a library assistant.

GENERAL RULES TO FOLLOW
WHEN USING THE LIBRARY

1. No eating, no drinking sodas or any type of liquids and no gum chewing.
2. No radios or noisy games.
3. No cell phone use.
4. Always ask the library staff to help when you need assistance.
5. When you check books out of the library, keep them clean and return them on time, if your book is returned late you will be asked to pay a late fee so always find out when your date to return your book or your can recheck your book out again if you have not completed reading it.
6. You can also check out movies and CD's.
7. You must have a membership card, the cards are free, without a library card you can not check out item of any kind you can use the library with out a membership card. The library can be fun, educational and informative.

MANNERS AT THE MOVIES

1. Follow all exit rules.
2. Use your indoor voice.
3. Take your seat.
4. Turn cell phone off.
5. No playing around with your friends like hitting, talking loud.
6. Do not put your feet on back of the seats.
7. When you are finished with your popcorn, candy and soda containers put in the trash can when you are leaving the movie theater, not on floor.
8. When the movie is over leave the theater quietly.

MANNERS AND ETIQUETTE TO BE USED WHEN SHOPPING IN THE MALL

When out at the mall always have an adult or older sister or brother with you. It is not a safe idea to go to the mall alone. Never talk to strangers.

BE SAFE

1. Use your indoor voice
2. No eating in the stores
3. No running or playing in the mall or store
4. Use your table manners when eating and use your napkin
5. Always make sure you have an adult with you
6. Do not go into the store touching everything only items you plan to try on or buy.

ENJOY SHOPPING AT THE MALL

SLEEPOVER MANNERS AN ETIQUETTE

I am sure your parents know or have been introduced to your girlfriend's family that you are sleeping over.

Your parents should have the name, address and telephone number of the parent of your girlfriend. Let your parents know the time the sleepover starts and the time to pick you up the next day.

TAKE THE FOLLOWING ITEMS WITH YOU.

1. Wash cloth, towel and soap.
2. Tooth brush, tooth paste and mouth wash.
3. Deodorant
4. Body lotion
5. Hair care products
6. Your own pillow, blanket and stuff animal.
7. Sleep wear, pajamas and a robe, you will need slipper or socks.
8. Take a clean change of clothes, underwear, and top clothes. Take money with you if you all are planning an outing the next day.

Remember to use your indoor voice, use your table manners.

Be respectful at your friend's home, knock on all doors before entering makes sure you get a come in before entering the room.

Be friendly and sociable to other guest.

Do not ask personal question. Do not open the refrigerator without permission

THE MEANING OF ETIQUETTE

Etiquette is a French word that means ticket. During ceremonial activities in the Royal Court of France everyone was given etiquette (tickets). These tickets were the rules governing the Royal Ceremonies.

The tickets let the people know what to do and where to stand in the court yard. They were not allowed to stand on the grass.

In 1750 word etiquette entered the English language meaning a set of rules that society wants us to use so that we treat people with respect and honesty.

Etiquette has to do with good manners. It is not so much our own manners, but making sure other people feel comfortable by the way we treat them.

CIVILITY SKILLS

Civility means polite in a formal way. A polite act, acts of speaking kindly, courteous acts and expressions.

SOME COMMON COURTESIES

1. saying you are sorry shows a concern for other people.
2. Saying thank you is good manners.
3. A smile and saying good morning is good and it makes people around you feel good.
4. Cover your mouth when you cough or sneeze. Make sure you use a tissue and wash your hands.
5. Do not comb or brush your hair in public.
6. When you have to pass gas, hold it until you can excuse yourself, if you cannot hold it, let it out and be ready to own up and apologize.
7. be honest.
8. be considerate
9. be kind.
10. Speak with a kind tone and voice.

COMMON COURTESY IN PUBLIC PLACES

You can never stop being aware of your behavior in public places, remember you are being observed by people and they will make a judgment or form an opinion of your conduct and behavior.

When you are out in public be thoughtful, respectful and aware of the feelings others.

BEHAVIOR IN
PUBLIC PLACES

When eating out in a restaurant always use proper table manners, remember to use your napkin. Chew with mouth closed. Use your indoor voice talk about pleasant things make sure your conversation is good to talk about while dining.

Do not eat from someone else plate, ask the server for a small plate the food can be put on the small plate and then eaten.

If you have a need to go to the bathroom, just excuse yourself do not announce that you need to use the bathroom just go, always wash your hands before and after you use the toilet.

LET THERE BE VIRTUES

NEGATIVE GESTURES IN PUBLIC PLACES

There is some negative gesture you should avoid in public

1. Excessive scratching of your head in public is unsanitary.
2. Laughing at others hurts their feelings.
3. Talking in church disturbs and it is disrespectful to other worshiper especially when the pastor is preaching.
4. Talking in the movie can be annoying to other movie guest.
5. Never point or stare at people.
6. Sneezing and not covering your mouth is unhealthy to the people around you they could catch your germs.
7. Picking your nose is disgusting to others and is unsanitary.
8. Picking your ears is very unpleasant to others.
9. Yawning with your mouth wide open is not pleasing to anyone's eyes.
10. Do not whisper in front of people, it might make them think you are talking about them it is rude and makes a person feel bad.
11. Gossiping is unkind and hurtful it is usually untrue.
12. Do not comb or brush your hair in public.
13. Do not put on lipstick or apply make up in public.
14. Never stand close to people when you are in public places, do not get in others people's space, stand at least and arm distance from a person when in line in the bank, store, school, church and all public places or when you are just standing talking to the person.

PLEASE ALWAYS ACT LIKE A WELL MANNERED YOUNG LADY IN PUBLIC PLACES.

CULTURAL AWARENESS

It is good manners to respect people from different cultural backgrounds. A person's culture is based on and defined by history. Their culture is their belief in custom, religion, food the way they dress, the language they speak, and communication styles.

In the United States we greet by saying 'hello' and shaking hands. However, in some countries they do not shake hands, but might bow to each other. In some cultures, men do not shake hands with women. In other cultures, men and women do not sit together during worship service.

Today we live in a multicultural society. If you have a friend or classmate that is from different culture than yours, introduce him or her to your culture and he or she will share things about their culture.

If you want information about your culture, ask your mother, father, grandmother, grandfather, aunts and uncles, they are good resources. It is wonderful experience to learn about another person's culture.

COMMUNICATION SKILLS

Being able to communicate effectively helps build relationships, leadership and positive self-esteem. Communication is a way information is exchanged between individuals through a common system of symbols, sings, or behavior or verbal or written messages.

Learning how to communicate effectively is very important.

There are many ways we can communicate.

1. Verbal "talking"
2. Signs and symbols
3. Listening
4. Body language
5. Reading
6. Writing
7. Computers
8. Cell phones
9. telephone

Verbal Communication

When talking to others always speak clearly so you can be heard and understood. Look at the person when you are talking. Be careful of how you respond verbally to others because you can never take an unpleasant word back. When talking beware of the tone of your voice.

When having a conversation with friends be sure to pick good topics to talk about. Do not talk about issues that will make you and your friends uncomfortable. If you get into a conversation learn to tactfully disagree and end the conversation. Cultural differences can get misunderstood at times.

Public Speaking

When you speak in public always know the subject matter that you are speaking about. Speak loudly and clearly. Make eye contact with your audience. You will have the opportunity to do public speaking at school, giving reports in the classroom and in church. If you belong to a social or sporting organization you will also get a chance to speak in public. You will feel nervous about standing and speaking in front of an audience. The more you speak you will develop a comfort level.

SIGNS AND SYMBOLS

When you see certain signs and symbols you know exactly what they mean.

Example: when you see a red stop sign it means stop, a golden arch is the McDonald sign, there are many signs in sporting games that communicate to the people what is going on in the game.

LISTENING

Listening is a great way to communicate. Listening is to hear with thoughtful attention and consideration. When someone is talking do not talk at the same time, listen then make your comments. It is rude to cut a person off before they finish what they are saying, you can learn a lot by being a good listener. When you do make a comment on what has been said you can agree or disagree tactfully (without a argument).

COMMUNICATION SKILLS

BODY LANGUAGE

Body language is an important communication skill, 95 % of communication is body language. Your body and gestures can tell people a lot about your feeling.

Example: Not making eye contact can mean that you are shy or not telling the truth.

Making eye contact when you are talking to a person is a positive communication skill.

Holding your shoulder's up shows confidence and good posture.

When you walk slowly it appears that you are lazy, walking briskly appears that you are confident and have a destination.

Arms crossed over your chest and hand's tucked inside makes you appear defensive and indifferent.

Hand's above the waist is positive. Hand's on your hip is a negative and a demanding position.

When both feet are on the floor we look alert and responsive.

When you are shaking your feet and legs it makes you appear nervous and less confident.

Fidgeting shows that you are nervous when you are moving from side to side when sitting in a chair.

When you are standing near or next to a person give them space, a forearm length away from the person. Stand eighteen to twenty-four inches from the person.

Example: when in a line at the store, bank, church, school, social affairs remember not to stand in a person's space, never touch a person without their permission, it rude and offensive to someone if you put your hands on them.

Now you can understand how very important body language is, people can read your body, so be careful not to send negative body language.

READING

Reading is a good communication skill, we read on a daily basis. We learn to read at an early age. We read signs, we read to follow directions on putting games together we learn to read to play games. We read the names of our favorite movies, TV programs and labels on foods. We read street signs, we read books for school and enjoyment at home we read our homework assignments so we can complete the homework. Reading is a skill that helps us learn to communicate more effectively. We learn to spell so we can read the better we spell the better we will read, the dictionary is very helpful in the correct way to spell a word it gives the meaning of the word and how to pronounce the word correctly.

WRITING

Writing is a good way to communicate, letters, invitations, thank-you-notes, books and newspapers. Thank-you-notes are always hand written when someone gives you a gift, invited you out to a dinner or allowed you to stay in their home. Thank you notes are personal and must be hand written and sent through the postal service not through an email.

Example of a thank-you-note, it can be short and sweet, not long and fancy.

To Aunt Ann,

Thank you for the blue necktie. Each time I wear it I will think of you. My new necktie reminds me of a tie that President Obama was wearing on TV last week. He wears the best blue neckties. I also have a dark blue suit that I can wear my necktie with.

Thanks, Nephew Tommie

THE COMPUTER

A computer is an electronic machine capable of accepting data at a high speed and showing or printing the results. This makes communication easier, faster and very informative many homes have computers, workplace, schools and colleges have computers for your use. Computer are the fastest form of communication we can get in touch with the world, face book, email and much more. Be very careful about the personal information you put into the computer it can cause a lot of problems for you in the future so use your computer wisely.

Telephone Manners

When you answer the telephone at home, greet the caller by saying hello. The caller will ask to speak to the person they are calling. Let that family member know that she or he has a call, use your indoor voice it would be rude to yell loudly to that family member that has a call. If family is not home, take a message, if the caller wants to leave a message. Write the name of the caller, number, time, date and any message. Give it to your family member when they return home.

Cell Phone

Cell phones are a big part of communication. Some parents provide their children with cell phones. It is a necessary form of keeping in touch with your parents, especially if everyone has a busy schedule. Cells phones are not toys and should only be used for important matters and only in places that allow the use of cell phones. Do not use your cell phone in school, work, hospitals, some public transportation and stores will ask you not use your cell phone when their service is being used.

This is how you make and introduction.

Make sure you always introduce people that do not know each other.

When being introduced

1   Always stand
2   Always smile.
3   Make eye contact.
4   Extend your right hand for a handshake, it is a friendly thing to do and this is the way we greet each other in the U.S.A.
5   Say something friendly like "It is nice to meet you or how are you doing?
6   Repeat the person's name.

INTRODUCING SOMEONE TO A GROUP

You say I want you all to meet James my next door neighbor, each person will introduce herself or himself.

RULES OF MAKING AN INTRODUCTION

Always introduce a younger person to an older person, say the name of the older person first.

Example: Aunt Ann this is my friend Jiamond, Jiamond this is my Aunt Ann.

You always introduce the higher status person first.

Example: Lt. Van, meet Sgt. Stacy, Sgt. Stacy meet Lt. Van.

ALWAYS INTRODUCE A MAN TO A WOMAN AND A BOY TO A GIRL.

EXAMPLE: Victoria this is Amos, my classmate, Amos this is Victoria my new church friend. Males always stand when being introduce to a female.

HERE ARE THE MOST IMPORTANT THINGS TO REMEMBER WHEN MAKING AN INTRODUCTION

The most important person comes first. A person of greater importance would be considered such by rank, by position, by age (people having higher authority) or gender, in a social situation a women, especially and older woman's name would be stated first.

Example: Mrs. Obama, (important person) I would like to introduce Mr. James (less important person). You can add some background information this is a good way to start a conversation. When you make the introduction, say something interesting about the person, nothing that is personal or embarrassing.

Example: introducing a boy to a girl

Jazmine this is Troy my friend from school, his goal is to write a book. Troy this is my friend, Jazmine she goes to my church.

The custom of handshaking goes back to early times in human history to a time of self-preservation when, according to the book, "The Custom OF Mankind" Copyright 1924 one savage fellow met another with whom he wished to be friendly, he held out his bare right hand the weapon hand––as a symbol, or sign, of peace––the other fellow understood––they joined forces hunting, eating, and probably living together in the same cave.

A handshake is the way we greet people in America. When we meet someone for first time we always shake hands and give a nice verbal greeting, like it is a pleasure to meet you.

When shaking hands, extend your right hand in a vertical position with your thumb pointing upward, and your fingers together, the web and index finger to meet the web of the other person's hand. Do not shake a person's hand to hard just give a firm hand shake, 2 or 3 shakes, let the person give a greeting before you stop the handshake. Always stand, smile, speak and make eye contact. Women, girls, men and boys shake hands the same way.

LET THERE BE VIRTUES

HANDSHAKE

A handshake is the way we greet people in America. When we meet someone for the first time we always shake hands and give a nice verbal greeting, like it is a pleasure to meet you.

When shaking hands, extend your right hand in a vertical position with your thumb pointing upward, and your fingers together, the web and index finger to meet the web of the other person's hand just give a firm hand shake, 2 or 3 shakes, let the person give a greeting before you stop the handshake. Always stand, speak and make eye contact. Girls, boys, women and men shake hands the same way.

You shake hands when:

1   when you are introduced to someone.
2   At the end meeting with someone.
3   After an interview.
4   When you meet someone you know and have not seen in a while.
5   When saying good bye to a friend or acquaintance.

TABLE MANNERS

Having good table manners are important; they are good social skills to have. When you have good table manners your friends will enjoy eating with you. You must use good table manners when you are eating at home, a friends house, or public eating places,

Prior to beginning your meal, place a napkin in your lap. When eating, keep one hand in your lap and your feet on the floor so you don't kick the person across from you. Always use good posture at the dining table: sit up straight, hold your head up, and bring your food to your mouth.

Be sure to place small bites of food in your mouth, not large bites. Drink your liquids slowly in small sips.

The correct way to butter your bread is to break off a small piece of bread and butter it. You will have a small plate to put your bread on. Only touch the piece of bread that you will be eating.

When you are eating soup, spoon the soup away from you. Never blow your soup and do not make the mistake of slurping your soup loudly.

1. Never rest your elbows on the table while eating.
2. Chew with your mouth closed.
3. Do not talk with food in your mouth.
4. Do not blow your nose while others are eating; It could spoil someone's appetite. Go to the bathroom to blow your nose, and then wash your hands with soap and water to prevent the spread of germs. When you return to the table, do not announce the reason you left the table.
5. Cover your mouth with a napkin when you cough or sneeze.
6. Do not pick your teeth with a toothpick.

Manners Do's

1. Wash your hands before eating your meal or before sitting down at the table.
2. Do wait for the blessing of the meal to be said before eating or drinking any part of your meal.
3. Use your indoor voice at the dining table.
4. Talk about pleasant things at the table.
5. Use your napkin, place your napkin on your knee, open the napkin near your lap not on top of the table.

6. If you sneeze cover your nose and mouth with your napkin.
7. If you leave the table, place your napkin to the left of your place setting, so that the soiled part is covered.
8. Use your fork, hold it like you hold your pencil.
9. Your spoon is used for soup, ice cream, Jello, apple sauce, and pudding.
10. When you are cutting your meat cut off one bite size piece, eat it, don't cut up your whole piece of meat.
11. When you have gravy break off a piece of bread, pick the bread up, use your fork, push the bread around in the gravy then put into your mouth.
12. Do pass the salt and pepper at the same time, even if the person only ask for one item.
13. When you butter your bread break off a piece of the bread, butter it eat that piece. Do not butter your entire piece of bread.
14. The correct direction to pass food at the table is to the right. When passing the food to the right the person can accept with their right hand.
15. If you drop your fork or spoon on the floor in a restaurant ask for another, leave the fork or spoon on the floor, if you pick it up do not put it on the table. If you drop your napkin you can pick it up.
16. When you start your meal use the eating utensils that is farthest away from your plate, first.

TABLE MANNERS DON'TS

1. Do not talk with food in your mouth.
2. Do not chew with your mouth open.
3. Takes small bites of food do not stuff your mouth with food.
4. When drinking liquids take small slips do not gulp your drink down.
5. Do not talk about things that will gross people out.
6. Do not eat off another person plate, ask the server for a small plate and place the food on a plate.
7. Do not put your elbows on the table when eating a meal.
8. Do not kick the person sitting in front of you at the table keep your feet on the floor.
9. No singing at the table.
10. Keep your elbows to your side while you cutting up your meat.
11. Dip your soup spoon away from you do not blow your soup.
12. Do not blow your nose at the table, excuse yourself and go to the bathroom then wash your hands. You do not tell the guest at the table you had to blow your nose, just sit down and continue your meal. It would be rude to talk to about you blowing your nose.

THE PLACE SETTING

The way the forks, knives, spoons, glasses, cups, plates, bowls and napkins are arranged on the table cloth or placemat is called "a place setting".

The plate is in the center the napkin and the fork on the left of the plate, the knife and spoon are placed on the right, the glass is above the knife to the right.

BASIC TABLE SETTING

You will have many occasions to set the table. It's always good manners to offer assistance in setting the table. Always wash your hands before setting the table.

The plate of each setting is placed in the middle of the setting.

The knife is placed on right next to the plate with the blade inwards.

The spoon is placed facing up to the right of the plate next to knife.

The forks are on the left, with their prongs facing up.

The napkin is on the left or placed in the center of the plate.

Glasses and cups are placed above the plate on the right side, above the tip of the knife.

Your place setting should only be set for the number of people eating the meal.

HOW TO USE THE CLOTH NAPKIN

1. Place the napkin in your lap with the folded edges toward your knee.
2. Do not open your napkin on the table top. Unfold the napkin on your lap.
3. Leave your napkin on your lap until you are finished your meal.
4. Use your napkin to dab your mouth after eating or drinking a liquid.
5. Your napkin also keeps food and stains off your clothes.
6. When you sit down for your meal you can find your napkin in the center of the plate or to the left of the plate or displayed in a glass or on the plate, it is up to the hostess to place her napkins were she wants them.
7. When you leave the table to go to the bathroom you can place your napkin to the left of the plate or place napkin in your chair. Do not make a statement that you are going the bathroom, just say excuse me, it would be rude to say that you are going to the bathroom.
8. Never refold your napkin or place it on your plate after using.

PASSING THE FOOD IN THE RIGHT DIRECTION AT THE DINING TABLE

What is the correct direction to pass the food when you dining? Pass the food to the right. The reason for this rule is the great majority of people are right handed.

When you pass the food to the right the person can accept with their left hand and serve themselves with their right hand.

THE SALT AND PEPPER SHAKER

Do not reach across the table, do not stand up to reach the salt and pepper shaker ask the person sitting closest to the shakers to pass them.

The person passing the salt and pepper will pass both the salt and pepper at the same time that is the rule, it does not matter if the person only asked for the pepper you pass the salt also.

FOODS THAT ARE DIFFICULT TO EAT

Soup; use your spoon, never slurp your soup, do not blow your soup, and hold you're spoon like a pencil and away from you. Never leave your spoon in a soup bowl, dip soup away from yourself gently scraping the spoon across the back of the soup bowl to catch any drips. Never blow your soup, do not place your mouth to the soup bowl bring the soup and spoon up to your mouth.

The reason that you do not leave your spoon in your soup you could accidently hit the spoon, and cause the soup to spill on the person sitting next to you, or across from you causing stains to their clothing that would be embarrassing. The reason for not blowing your soup is the same reason it could blow on the table or the person sitting next to you.

Salads; cut up your salad with a knife and use a fork.

Peas; use your fork.

Lobster; use a crab cracker and a cocktail fork.

Spaghetti; use your fork.

Eat jello, ice cream and pudding with a spoon

THE FOLLOWING FOODS CAN BE EATEN WITH YOUR FINGERS

Bread, cookies, pizza, tacos, sandwiches, hotdogs, hamburgers, popcorn, corn on the cob, streamed shrimp, French fries, bacon, ribs, carrot sticks, chicken wings, chicken legs, celery sticks, pickles, grapes, apples, oranges, bananas, watermelon, cantaloupe, chips, and candy.

YOUR IMAGE/ PERSONAL APPEARANCE

First impressions are very important and often times the way you dress and your grooming can give people an impression of you. Always try to look your best. Remember if you dress sloppy it will make people think or get the impression that you do not care about yourself. You should dress in what makes you comfortable and what looks good on you.

Does what you wear really make a difference? Yes it does people in our society judge you by what you wear. So always make sure your outfit is color coordinated.

Dress appropriately; wear the right clothes for the occasion.

Everyday school wear -wear casual clothing sweaters, skirts, slacks, jeans, blouse and casual dress and everyday shoes.

Dressy wear- you should wear a dressy dress and dress up shoes, wear jewelry and a special fragrance.

Church wear-show respect to God by wearing clothes that are neat and clean, respectable clothing. No see thru tops or jeans with holes in them, make sure your clothing are pressed, the hem is intact, no tears in your clothes no missing buttons. Look your best.

Formal wear is wearing a long gown, when go to your prom, military ball, ring dance, dressy shoes and nice jewelry.

LET THERE BE VIRTUES

PERSONAL APPEARANCE

Your posture is important always sit up straight when sitting in a chair.

When sitting in a chair sit with your legs closed and ankles together or you can cross your legs above the knees, place your hand in your lap.

There is a proper way to sit down in a chair, place back of your knees to the chair and sit down lowering yourself in chair, do not wiggle back in chair.

Good posture includes the way you walk, walk straight glide smoothly, and moderate pace. Head up, not a lot of hip movement.

You should strive to look feminine, being proud that God made you a girl.

You should select clothing which is appropriate to the occasion. Never over dress or wear clothing that bring a lot attention to yourself.

PERSONAL HYGIENE
(CARE OF THE BODY)
YOUR BODY IS YOUR TEMPLE

You will need to bath daily using warm water and soap. A shower or bath makes you feel better and relaxes you. Keep your under arms clean and dry, always use deodorant to prevent under arm odor.

Change your under wear daily to prevent odor. It is not good manners or socially accepted not to keep your body clean. It is very offensive to other for you to have body odor, you must bath and change your under garments. You cannot put back on the same under garment without washing them.

Always brush your teeth in the morning and before going to bed. The dentist would like you to brush your teeth after each meal but is difficult to brush at school and other public places.

Keep your hair neat and clean and well groomed. Shampoo on regular basis and keep hair and scalp oiled. Your mother will help you keep your hair clean and neat. You might also have a beautician that you go to on regular appointment.

Keep your finger nail clean and trimmed, no chipped nail polish; use a nice soft girlie nail polish color.

Keep your toes nail trimmed and feet clean and dry, change your socks daily and wash your tennis shoes on regular basis to prevent foot odor.

Always use a good soap and lotion on your skin.

LEADERSHIP SKILLS

Leaders have the ability to work well with others that have a vision and all work toward a common goal.

Leaders have the ability to influence people and delegate responsibility. Leaders set a good example and they lead by example. A good leader must be honest, have good manners and have good communication skills. Leaders are respectful and use good judgment, and they think before they speak. They are well groomed and have great social skills.

23RD PSALM

The Lord is my Shepherd, I shall not want.

He maketh me to lie down in green pastures. He leadeth me beside the still waters.

He restoreth my soul; he leadeth me in the paths of righteousness for his name sake.

Yea, though I walk through the valley of the shadow of death, I will fear no evil, for thou art with me, thy rod and thy staff they comfort me.

Thou preparest a table before me in the presence of mine enemies thou anointest my head with oil, my cup runneth over.

Surely goodness and mercy shall follow me all the days of my life and I will dwell in the house of the Lord forever.

Amen

Made in the USA
Middletown, DE
12 December 2021

55229844R00031